Also by Joseph Donahue

Before Creation
Monitions of the Approach
World Well Broken
Incidental Eclipse
Terra Lucida
Dissolves
Red Flash on a Black Field
Dark Church
Wind Maps I–VII
The Disappearance of Fate

JOSEPH DONAHUE

INFINITE CRITERIA

ISBN: 978-1-7363248-8-2

BSE Books are distributed by
  Small Press Distribution
  1341 Seventh Street
  Berkeley, CA 94710
  orders@spdbooks.org | www.spdbooks.org
  1-800-869-7553

BSE Books can also be purchased at
www.blacksquareeditions.org and www.hyperallergic.com

Contributions to BSE can be made to
  Off the Park Press, Inc.
  976 Kensington Ave.
  Plainfield, NJ 07060
  (Please make checks payable to Off the Park Press, Inc.)

To contact the Press please write:
  Black Square Editions
  1200 Broadway, Suite 3C
  New York, NY 10001

An independent subsidiary of Off the Park Press, Inc.
Member of CLMP.

Publisher: John Yau
Editors: Ronna Lebo and Boni Joi
Design & composition: Shanna Compton

Cover art: Xylor Jane, "92277" (2017), 20 × 14½ inches, oil
on board. Courtesy of the artist and Parrasch Heijnen, Los
Angeles, from the collection of William Lazarus.

for Geoffrey O'Brien

At heart, you are
a disgusting beggar,
a slave to desire
        —Taneda Santōka
            (trans. Burton Watson)

Contents

13   Infinite Criteria

41   In My Window, a Heart-Shaped Prism

49   The Red Gate

59   Even as Earth

71   A Row of Solar Panels in a Field

91   The Logic of It All

105 Done Died One Time

131 Clouds of the Realm Above

144 Acknowledgments

145 About the Author

INFINITE CRITERIA

INFINITE CRITERIA

Such whiskey as pours
infinity down all
throats

Storm tipping sideways
the ocean caroms
into air

On a mountain, a depressive
He claims cities are
less than mist

Exacting glance,
admonishing
amour

Flayed, it would seem,
to where bones
break apart

The ocean rising
as the plane
drops

Copy, then, in secret,
the damning
emails

✫

Dawn: empty
wheelchair, icy
parking lot

Would these descending walls
were of pearl, beryl,
or feldspar

Having survived the night
unfilled, the fresh
pit glistens

The sun flaring,
but the ice
darkening

Hands to ground
Cry out to
the sky

The black clouds are curtains drawn
through day, twilight,
and the night

The treetops
show what's coming,
as do the roots

✧

Once a school playground,
now just rebar in
a raw maw

An origami Titanic
in a puddle,
a paid bill

One beauty birthed
another. Both now
sip mimosas

✡

The clear sky
shines. Plums rot
under a tree

The shadow is
a chapel designed
by a suicide

Either winter is arriving
or a fever. Awake,
shivering

A father sips wine from a can
while a troubled
son talks

The street ends
at the river. The water
is whipped up

The mind
is like heaven—
All's over, all at once

But for titanium screws
from the neck, down,
I'm dead

☆

A face that says
my son has messed up bad
and I can't help him

A face that says
my hope is so high it hurts
me and cripples me

A face that says
I may be Dorothy
but this is not Oz

Kids in costumes
holding out bags, door
to motel door

A boy with an axe-
halved head,
laughing

Yet another Halloween
your parents in
their ditch

Back when this
motel was a hospital
for white folks

✡

Such metaphysics
as mesmerize
the dying

Early light
Trashcan at the curb,
the rim, brilliant

Life and light
weaken. High up,
a hawk, maybe an owl

What do I do
all day with only
a speechless child to talk to

An umbrella
in flames, outside
a synagogue

After the lightning strike
the boy bleeds from
the ears

Obstreperous
clasp, a slinky
necklace

Further
into the forest
the train's one note

☆

Hide from
the light, then
darken your mind

The bee hangs at
the cusp of the flower,
then drops

No lips in
the midst of
words I want to hear

Glory fails. The
light wanes
in shame

Ghoulish has-beens
vetted for high
office

Hidden flames howl,
chained inside
the sun

Birds—
silent, in
thinning vines

Victorious,
a hate group rolls by
in silky billows

✡

Doorway at night,
scent of unseen
roses

A gift in a dream—
parental ashes inside
an Easter egg

That we die
makes us just like
Jesus

Days, torn
apart, nights
not made whole

A circle of the young
A ball bouncing
among them

A red, raw streak
Her neck where she tugs
on her necklace

Kids and the old
afraid to step out on
icy earth

When birds die
do their bodies turn
into song?

✡

Cruel clouds,
the sun's ruined
orgasm

The sky blues the window
of what otherwise
is all brick

The beating
deepens: bones
bruise with each blow

(Anyone else would be
humiliated
by now)

No roses
that night, yet
the air was sweet

✡

A motel
less for lovers
than for outpatients

A lobby
less for luggage
than for oxygen tanks

Blood thinner
—he's wise not
to shave

Suicidal,
but to the
world, a wit

A sky clear and blue
but fading into
white

☼

A motel less
about ease than
about the infinite

Roof shingle
auras of gray,
plum, teal

Prepped for nightsticks
the protesters
exult

Across from the clinic,
no surprise, the
mortuary

Moon, huge,
wants to come back
to a hole now all ocean

Shivering from cold
as, once, from
pleasure

Sky the
color of ice yet
the sun is still burning?

☼

Two girls talk as they walk
Path dust, sea froth
Wet hems

A once acclaimed scholar
doubled over, gasping,
in a dumpster

Thugs at a motel breakfast table
at dawn, talking
about dogs

A quiet road that
keeps washing
out to sea

Reflected on the
window, the
brick wall

The distinguished
get old. The old
are ghouls

✡

Pull me apart
and in my bleeding
see creation out of nothing

Down the road
teargas, water cannons,
on and off screams

A brain artery
opens, new thoughts
flood me

The land is flat
The clouds are flat
Far off, both are ablaze

Such delight as had
hoped to remain
unknown

The bird gone now
but the spot
forever a perch

The topmost
cloud does not lie,
the sun is orange-gold

You appear safe
yet you are
plundered

✡

Sunrise lasting till night
all that is rose-colored
goes black

Police pulling up
behind you as
you text

The Earth
rounds the sun
trailing a victory banner

On the sheet, lipstick kisses
where the heart
would be

The clot need not be
where the pain
appears

Above the crematory
spirits reminisce
about bliss

✣

The molecules that gather
to be you have a fate
beyond you

Dropping to the ground
the sky turns
a dull silver

What was never done
yet now seems
undone

Long skid of clouds:
the sun got
T-boned

Dreams still being
what feels real about
waking life

Handprints on the headboard
A previous guest's
wild ride

To clouds
streaming into fire, say:
Don't be afraid

Each on the path is lost,
path rising to where
mist drops

A face that says a punch
might just deepen
my ideals

Magnetic waves pouring
from a storage closet
A migraine

Uncommonly low
and dark clouds
flooding in

A face that says I'm spiraling inward
and down, while you just
keep talking

The highway gets
hysterical. The coastline,
trembling

A face that says all this is dreamed
by a woman asleep
in Jerusalem

✡

Giddy in the elevator,
descending to the wedding,
bridesmaids

The water recedes
Houses, rising, not to be
lived in again

All things arrive here
in a form, and keep
it for a while

Those loved, all
leaving, stepping down
a long stair

✡

A face that says
I feel what a rivet feels
holding together a ship at sea

A face that says sad to see the bus
flash past full of kids
going to school

A brick wall all day
Toward evening,
a butterfly

A face, mere minutes
out of the womb, that says:
I have my doubts

Those chars
were once a door
gone through many times

The sky feels
the pull of other planets
and would leave

Fruit of a once scandalous
romance burbling
in the car seat

✡

We were all just shadows
You the first of us to
seep into night

The cars behind the train
are all black and
full of stones

Wheelchairs,
air tanks, masks
Motel lobby breakfast

A mind
wired to never
understand itself

So huge a moon,
not again till
I'm gone

✿

A face that says I feel like a schoolgirl
puzzled by the power of
her own beauty

A face that says I kneel to what-
ever cuts my head
from my body

Smoke from afar
that says nothing
far is left

A face that says nothing reaches me
I am like the inside
of a brick

☼

Motel lobby all
wedding guests and
outpatients

Like hospitals in China so
crowded folks stand
in line to die

The sun gives up
and the sky
goes gray

A face that says after a dream of
surgical implants I wake
god forsaken

Too fine to be seen,
a rainfall felt
on the palm

An hour ago
wild sex but now
guests at a memorial

Glowing juice
drunk through
a portal in the neck

A face that says even the cruel
endure needless
suffering

✡

First horse slaughtered
on an altar in the Indus valley
Thou art that

The line where light ends
as night flows after the falling sun
Thou art that

A driveway under a night sky,
weeping all round, joyful
Thou are that

Back when this motel was a hospital
the death in this room
Thou are that

—years, your father, not
calling him, the phone, right there
Thou are that

Sexy, in black mesh
Tomorrow, in for surgery
Thou art that

Nothing to be said
No one left to hear it
Thou art that

✲

As if the Angel
of Death took you
and no one noticed

Lessening light
is more intimate and
not adverse to shadows

A kiss too full on
the lips to be
pro forma

The trembling of
the veil. Or so they
used to say

Death slips a blue-beaded bracelet
off her wrist. Swallow
it, she says

8 or 9 beads
at a time, then the
gold thread, the clasp

The depths of hell
pale through the day,
but then, night comes back

✡

Not so much
a church as a motel
where men have sex with horses

All is only touched once,
and only by light
and rainwater

Finally, the trees
catch up with the season
They glow with their own oblivion

Asceticism only lasting
till nightfall, then
it’s carnival

Nation where
jackals oversee policy
and snakes mind the details

A tribunal of
withered tongues,
earthly justice

Panic attacks
audible despite
the pillow

Feeling far off,
as if atop a mountain
pondering impermanence

☆

Right after that wall
infinity goes
all blue

Then a sky like paint store samples
in subtle
grades of black

Past the police car
a boy wrapped in a blanket
crouching on a curb

Such hopelessness
only a gasp is
appropriate

The sun lifts the night like
the lid of a box
I wake inside of

All falls dark
yet the sky shines
What was that thought you had?

IN MY WINDOW A HEART-SHAPED PRISM

IN MY WINDOW A HEART-SHAPED PRISM

The prism
shaped like a heart
shreds any approach of pure light

My glory will be
to blossom just before
the final freeze

Water torn
in silver rings
as a train passes

Further puzzled, now, by
a footbridge not there
when I left

Butterflies
above a field
were once dead infants

High in the black
above the thin crescent,
pulsing junk

Were so much not so
they would be falling in love
while talking

Turn out the
office light and sit
on the floor beside the desk

Like snow in a shaken globe
but the flakes are red—
Blood in the eye

I wanted to slip
into the earth so I
tweaked my dosage

I wanted to slip
into the earth but
my sisters intervened

I wanted to slip
into the earth and drift far
down into the fire

This dreaming
does not wait for
eyes to close, mind to wander

☼

The world has gone sideways
The animals are
in awe

Never yet so awake
as when stepping out
into this barrage

Rippling pool
momentarily
turquoise

Left in the door
overnight: the key,
gold in morning sun

(That makeup
means: chemo,
again)

House sold,
one last party
for those departing

Early spring:
outside the jail
a dog barks at a bird

✳

Rain so bright
it could be snow
turning to rain

A morning so dark
it could be night
never left

A noon so dark
hard to say you've
been awake

☼

No need not to die
the sun tells the
fleeing light

THE RED GATE

THE RED GATE

The frosted fur of deer at dawn
sleeping in the woods
—prismatic

Bird shadows
fly through the grass
Any next gust could be wet

Coked-out in a dream
your brain a hive of
happy bees

A barn filled with
broken pianos and called
an academy

Her question,
a head shot to
my hope

Now with dismay moans
one who once did so
in delight

✩

So much the sun suffers to see
yet forbears
to burn

No way to slip across
gravel quietly
at night

It was a time in my life,
she said, I needed
sex every day

My clit, then, was like
a morsel of pear
inside a cake

All while deer
gnawed a field down
from green to raw stone

Magnolia leaves
pulling the sky's gray
into their green

☼

A sunrise more about falling
away than rushing
toward

A flight attendant
is missing her past life
as a prison guard

Hand, dried blood,
a cut from unlocking
the gate at night

Red gate
rain-soaked,
death beyond it

Gate painted red
in memory of my days
as a Maoist

☼

No back to go back
to, they're not
alive, now

Between the chirps,
as heard in the
fluttery lull

Not, then,
sobbing, a hacked
computer on her lap

Wanting this life
so much I wound up
in the hospital

The red gate
pried wide
the lock in pieces

The stars
make me sad so
I look away

☼

It's like after getting slain
in the spirit yet all is
just the same

30,000 feet in the air,
still unclear why you
left the house

✵

You feel robbed yet
uncertain what
was taken

A salamander leaps
up at the door
as it opens

The need, then,
to desist, to cede,
to de-access, to drop

Field, desolate
The deer must be
deep in the woods

Parents joyful with
each other
as not in life

✡

Drops spark
along the white rail,
on steps of soaked boards

Rail gone,
cop cars, flashing
So, too, a firetruck

Perfect bodies,
veneration their due,
pass through the dying world

Girls in earbuds jog
through falling
leaves

EVEN AS THE EARTH

EVEN AS THE EARTH

Even as the earth
turns in agony—
petals shine

She sits legs apart,
in a short skirt, on a hill
The wind reaching for her womb

A boy amazed at his
new sneakers, looks down at
his feet as he jumps up

Tree, turn
our dirty breath
pure

Apologies,
never to be said,
mouthed in a dream

✵

Dead ivy
clings to the tree
The tree drinks in sunlight

"I can't stop . . ."
Sinks into sobs
A night otherwise quiet

Above the parking lot
a coppery red
love god

A dinner-table glance
Immediate
misery

The way the clouds say:
Forsake all else,
enter the air

The way the creek says:
Leave here. Reach
the sea

The way the sun says:
I no longer hide
the final heat

✼

Flush summer forest
The dead tree
looks free

The ethically
retrograde know
what's coming

Sun pouring down,
spine unknotted, floating
on your back in a swimming pool

Dumpster spilling
shreds of what was
a bedroom

Once, greatly loved,
now, morally
monstrous

Light so pale, as if
the sun had seen the day
and took fright

Totaling
the car I went home
and lay down in the dark

Sent by sleep among
the many once
alive

☼

The talk turns to
a hidden planet,
beyond Pluto

Sunlight touches,
consumes, and abandons
the wall farthest from the window

Alone but never
so, so many close by,
in the heart

A passing train
The tinsel on the
lobby tree trembles

.

☼

Dead girl points to
birds in the sky while
other kids play

The dead siblings pose
behind the living,
no less alive

Dead infants
propped lifelike
in their mothers' lap

Black awnings
make the shop not
too inviting

In a dream, your father
shows where to sign
a legal form

A woman touches an ache,
wipes blood from
her fingertips

New boots
beside the couch,
ankles a raw ring

The wings
all go still at once
The flock glides

A freighter sheathed in ice
On the horizon,
the sun

Hotel roof:
Bridesmaids ripple
From the hills, a breeze

Amidst ire,
the startle of
sudden affection

A grumpy salesperson
warms to the
customer

Face gashed
by a wrong way
bicyclist

At the bank
a past love turns,
says: I'm still waiting

☼

Deep in the earth
a train breaks down
All sit, silent

Not so much
looking at the painting
as feeling light pour through it

A mountain range
seen through a screen door
as the sun drops

Incarnations ago,
on a toboggan, her arms
ringing my waist

Let a crown of ice be
set on my head
in derision

David Bowie seeing
what the year would be
wrote *Black Star*

Would this were
the headwaters of the Amazon,
and me, hallucinating

Through the mouths of
multitudes,
a single misery

The womb
that bore me,
now loam

I've been called
to Florida. My mother
is losing her mind

✡

A sun-god hammers
gold sheets, hangs
them in the sky

Once a body stops,
the world has
never been

Two of the three
talk past each other
The third nods

A gleam flows
over stones, dirt, ice,
bounces back to the sky

Sopping dog,
the car smelling
like a cave of wolves

3 or 4 doors lean against a wall
window frames not yet
installed

Once-
loved faces
flash before waking

Case worker with a legal pad
awaiting your
deposition

The 25 billion other
places in space
life might be

A bowl on a shelf
too high for the one
chopping fruit

A ROW OF SOLAR PANELS IN A FIELD

A ROW OF SOLAR PANELS IN A FIELD

The here, where you'd
say you are, admits
no witness

Amid the hesitancies of night
a downpour
Now all glows

Each at a distance
from any other and each
facing a wall

In waking life, no daughter,
but here, warm tears
stream down

Prison visions
burned, the world
goes guideless

Yes, you look happy
in that photo, but then
you remember

A special gym
Aching skeletons,
many in casts

I am a parrot mortified
by its costume and
ludicrous hat

✷

The evacuees
bid adieu to their hosts
and head back to the holocaust

The clouds part
The realms above
stay hidden

Inside a seed,
which molecule
stirs first?

A stifled love cry
offered, toward evening,
to one far away

Dark when you slept,
darker still, when
you wake

In a parking lot
at night looking for
a cell phone

✡

Church roof solar
panels wedged into
red clay tiles

Dies at night,
is reborn next day
as a champagne foal

Hope for a late last
love ever lessening
as fate unfolds

Paws claw the floor above
The dogs are eager
to disinter you

All's gone
in an instant,
even the sky

✿

Field of solar panels
tipped back: black stones
awaiting a chisel

The years it takes
in some such ocean for
waves to topple

An opaque hole
in the translucence
wins a gasp

Paints, inks, dyes,
crushed powders of
the last Paradise

Scorch of the boiling
at the first tip
of the pour

✡

Sulk, sun, in your
upstairs back room
Burn by yourself

It took a postcard
mailed from a death camp
to get me my passport

Dancers throw
themselves down
and bounce back

A culture dirt poor
in everything except
ritual patterning

All of us kids again,
in the car, going to
the movies

A head going
side to side in a vast
negation of all proposed

✧

Whipped by wind
the dogwoods bleed
blossoms

Woke up feeling like
a noted betrayer
in the Bible

A kind of calm
only won through
immense blood loss

The ache wakes first,
waits a while, then
rouses you

Not so often so
weeping in adult life
out of nowhere

Blossoms opening toward
you as if you were
of the light

Whatever the bird
might feel, his song
brings delight

☆

So transcendent
a Japan existing only in
a distraught mind

✫

A massive moon
ringed in red over
ink trees

Day so gray
what light there is
is a lie

Dogs
dumbfounded
by an invisible fence

☼

Each brother would complete
the other. Each feels
painfully halved

Only what is said
in a head in a dream
can be believed

Not quite offhand,
her use, to you,
of the word, *smut*

Sad then to see
last week's blossoms
washed down the gutter

✡

Pale purple petal
cluster in some
unearthly vineyard

I want to be run through
and gasping. I want to die
dismayed at my fate

Those at the heart of
an explosion simply
disappear

You, too, feel more like you are
passing out of existence
than deeply in it

Like a corpse singing
of a new life it has
no part in

Earth begs for
a drenching but the
clouds say no

Not so much amorous
as feeling a need
to be arrested

Not so much broken
as feeling a need
to be pierced

☆

Two suitors passed out
drunk in the pasture
behind the girl's house

Flash of light
sideways through
the deluge

The bird walks down the wet tree
trunk in a long
slow spiral

A hapless dad
with a bossy
daughter

So gentle the ache
that will be, in the end,
a medical ordeal

Little time left
for the much
to come

☼

To the five notes
the bird adds, only
once, a sixth

The branch a bony hand that
once offered you
blossoms

What can be seen
shines blue
atop the trembling

A millisecond
in the head, with them,
where they are now

The whole Bible
is excrement except
for *Revelations*

New roof, yet to be
A hole overhead,
all night

You ask your brother
for advice, but
he turns away

☼

In that you imagine
your corpse would be found
you cling to life

Ringed in glass
the flame reacts to
the air above it

The song of praise
the shadow has
for the light

The shadow
so close to the light
but not destroyed by it

The shadow
reminding the light of
a depth beyond it

✿

Only at a peal of
thunder do you think
oh, it's Good Friday

For a few moments
the entire world streams
and gleams

Humidity being
just airborne
grief

It's like the sky
wants to keep
dreaming

☼

As if asked to leave the theater
at the movie's
best part

The zealous dog
bloodies the edge of
a fake bone

The outermost edge of such
ideas being all
I can bear

As if to say to those back then
I see how lonely
you were

A ridge of pale
yellow-green moss
between the bare trees

A spooky, too-thin woman
on a black road with
a big white dog

✡

Crossing Manhattan
the hurricane tips the island
sideways

Old clothes thrown out,
suits once worn at
gravesides

You think you're awake
but you've never not
been asleep

The word the breeze brings
to the leaves
dismays the sun

A spirit touches
my forehead,
a thought

At my midnight none pray
with me, not even
the birds

☆

A photo
of a black hole but there
seem to be other colors inside it

God gives us
a ghostly world
but in dreams all is alive

A salamander
crossing the porch
in spasms

What else would, if seen
otherwise, be
of flame?

An owl is amazed at
its own sudden
wingspan

✡

Such adornment
being only for
dire eyes

She breaks out
the brightest of her
nail paints

Each finger and toe now
an emanation of
the divine

And the world—
empty bookcases
in a garage

(As if you are
a risen being not
otherwise to be touched)

THE LOGIC OF IT ALL

THE LOGIC OF IT ALL

Said to have shouted racial slurs
at a parking lot
attendant

Crawling,
crown shattered,
Nebuchadnezzar

Having learned
nothing yet somehow
more pained

A low, full moon
over the motel
chars

What
is shameful
composes the soul

Mist on a field
A day reluctant to
emerge

Within a shadow
the cross casts
a shadow

✧

Plastic champagne glass
atop roadside
scrub grass

Rambunctious
pooch pissing all
over the ammo pouch

Dawn brings a soft gold
glimmer to the fur of
grazing deer

A whole hospital wing for
people who just need
to breathe

So not to fret Mom
the hemorrhage goes
unmentioned

The satellite,
no tales left to tell,
plunges into Saturn

The jogger seems
flayed with each step,
like a herald in a tragedy

☼

Wildfires of
marital misery
turn Canada to ash

High up, leaves on alert
while the rest of the
tree sleeps

Lights are on
but the bar is closed
So: Where, now?

☼

A horse balks
at pulling the slaughtered
carcass off the trail

Clear quartz
atop a wet splay
of shining white

Quiet lightning
Red rain. Huge sky
A sealed grave

All that you prize
goes unwanted
elsewhere

Touches of blood
in the green. Autumn
is here, but hiding

The glories of
those gone make it
hard to get out of bed

Deer emanate
from the beyond,
then go back

☆

This is what you were
All you are now
is not

Raw sewage
in the basement of
the hospital

Days of
steady wind
The lake tips on its side

In heaven
you beg for this
to stop and it doesn't

Grazing, all
at once the deer
look up

All are saying
congrats. Silently
you gasp, oh no

✫

I'm from a place so deep in China
China doesn't know
it's there

Some percent of
any crowd is singing
inside their heads

At work early
So quiet, the sun not
yet touching the windows

A woman too
beautiful to be seen
by anyone not dreaming

With the second sip
the sky flows
and folds

Blazing clouds pour
over a rim
of mud

Were you a hound
you would bay
in disbelief

☼

All falling
at a constant rate
so no one feels the falling

Snow said to be
days away but then
these flakes

Forgiven
and deeply loved,
but not awake

✡

Where tips of
mountains wrinkle
the sun meanders into the air

My beauty will
teach you detachment
she said, over tea

A desolation,
now, the kind that
martyrs pass through

Afloat, as if on
a bed frame in an
abandoned prison

Thinking for a moment
your parents are
still alive

Night's
cold wakes you
In day's heat, sleep deepens

A shivering fit
but then the pine
needles are still

Some new Pentecost
possibly, but with
no apostles

✡

The sun hiding so
shade can glow at what
would be dawn

The pond a
black gleam in
a wounded hollow

Dawn bled out
By noon the sky had
a bluish hue

✸

That night, we both got
breathless, both
blushed

After the rain,
the forest stream bed
fills with an olive-green fervor

Her words
a boat that bears
you over the abyss

Broken by grief,
mouthing
old prayers

A good night kiss,
cold of the night air
on her scarf

✡

The scent of cinnamon
lingering long after
the dessert

Intercut
monochromatic planes
and you, ecstatic

Like trees looking down
at their storm-torn
branches

In a forest by a pool
water wreathed in
pollen, swirls

Between each
intimate contact
eons lapse

Had you chosen
otherwise, joy would
be streaming down your face

✩

A hospital, a prison,
a monastery or
a morgue

I feel I am on the
floor of the sea
looking up

The school bus slows
A lone girl, waiting
Early mist

DONE DIED ONE TIME

DONE DIED ONE TIME

Well, I done died one time
and I ain't gonna die no more
                              —Rev. Gary Davis

Too high and bright to cast shadows
the gloriously
dissipating clouds

Flayed, as you are,
deep in your indulgence,
by ascetic ideals

Crying, then, while saying,
"This is where he used to live . . ."
to strangers, in a dream

Wanting, for the
season of heat ahead,
a cold cave to crawl into

Never so awake
as when within it,
this dream

Now that I'm
the last alive they
drop by every night

It's like the Resurrection
It's like the 40 days
of pure life

✪

Finally, no one
can find you, shadows
deepen into the last night

Shadows welling up
from wetlands
The sun aloft

Shadows so deep
you're not yet back—
nearly noon

Not back,
gone into the blaze
of finality, of shadows

✩

Don't slight the day,
sings the bird,
night hides there

Ravished, later,
by an obscene love, in
a reverie now beyond recall

A ladder of kisses
lifting upward from
a left anklebone

Born a day later
you would have died
in Vietnam

The to and fro of light
and shade, a sky
so indecisive

Many yet to be
named. My memoir:
Graves I'm Stepping On

When you're old,
he said, not much
need to eat

Every night, through
the trees, fully lit,
a vacant house

Dreaming mind,
the Ark. The pillow
Mt. Ararat

Grief and guilt like
two beaten dogs
at your feet

Inside that locked
box there's
a clock

A spark from
an emanation that
got wrecked in the descent

☼

Long dead, the philosophy professor
who told me about
Chinese scroll painting

Desired, from a high perch, by
a woman turned, now,
into a bird

Clouds like a concert piano
in the rotunda of
a cancer clinic

Blackout blinds down all day
Her father was a cop on
the night shift

She's in sales at Lowe's:
"I really know how
to block light"

(The trees, too, beg to be
beaten. Wind, make
them wait)

☼

Graduates, throwing caps in the air
like they're ready
to die

The clouds are
bridesmaids in white
slowly stepping down the aisle

Every night
inside your head
The Ascent of Mt Carmel

Shaken awake
on a cloudy day
to help find sunglasses

A first leaf goes silver
in the gray, then all
brighten

✿

Of Eden, a gust, a glint,
a glimpse as the
gutters flood

In a desert-colored
dress a wedding
photographer

Her expert eye catches
a necklace faintly
twisted

A world all
gowns, veils,
and held poses

The clouds
an interlocking tier of
five birdbaths

In the shadows
a thirsty hummingbird back
from death

Return to a hometown
No blood kin there
no more

✡

I wanted to be well enough to walk
in the hospital gardens
but I'm dead

Under the Wellfleet jogger's
footfall, a whale's
jaw

Die in a rice paddy, they said
Or, play clarinet in the
marching band

What was so long sought for
now held in hand,
an empty bin

Brother
dead in prison,
kid sister murdered

(behind the tennis courts
he took a beating
in your stead)

Can't pry the sun
apart from
its light

✧

Above the warehouse
a Patmos of
gold cloud

Walking, then, like a prophet
hundreds of cuts on
bare feet

Quiet and rested, free
of the thrall of all thought
about Paradise

Even that kiss, given
late in life, after
long grief

✷

Such agony
as a river might feel
mere miles from the sea

A highly liquored concoction:
frozen copper cup,
crushed ice

The green goes
down in waves and
rebounds into a mountain

Receding bands
of pink and gold, the
rush of nothing

Turned out my brother was
on the train and I
sat beside him

✰

A soap bubble
wobbling above
a tugboat

Girl on a piling, barefoot,
back to the tides,
eyes closed

The ballet is neither
Nerval's *Aurelia*,
nor your life

So many presences
that waking just
obliterates

Aortic spasm,
a light, last kiss
before you sleep

✧

Streaks of sun-colored
cloud seem to lie
on the river

A celestial mantilla
tattered with small black
rips in the water

Think of this
whiskey, she said, as
a goddess pissing freely down your throat

Further from the window
in the cool of the
room's deep

Living as if
out of a suitcase
50 years

Deer descend from the dunes
to greet you in
the surf

Metal sheets
Pits in the street
Passing tanks

✧

Such was what was once
Now all are gone,
are nowhere

Imperceptibly, to you,
your shirt has advanced towards
the status of a rag

Blessed enough
not to breathe and
have it hurt

✵

The world shines at dawn
from rainfall unheard
in the night

Sunlight
cascading into
her cupped hands

The new bride,
having wept, opens
the door, eyes shining

☼

The outermost of the known planets
is what affects
you, now

Asleep facing afar,
dreaming of leaving
in a snowstorm

First in line at
the blood work lab
the nurse, sulky

A bad dream waiting for sleep,
the news waiting for the
TV to turn on

Eyes said
to show ancestral
suffering

A grandmother
executed in her kitchen
by Communists

The upper stories vanish
as shade rises and
the sun falls

Universal consciousness
touching all thought,
the third sip

Each in tears in turn taking a selfie
with their father's
corpse

At sunset, this the last
place light reaches
before fading

Black twine runs through the folds
of purple the Hudson,
rough, at twilight

Quiet stairwell
but for trash plunging
down the chute

Sky, river, ocean, land,
an empty pier
amid it all

A beauty turns
away in a dream
garbling a revelation

Bags packed
Good to go any
hour this all ends

✷

Out of the abyss
of river, sky, and night,
a party boat

Thousands mount
the train to the beach
as mermaids

Milling, ankle-deep,
chatting, sky pours
into the water

Over pickled tomatoes
young women share
dog videos

The Wonder Wheel
The Parachute Drop
The Slingshot

Back spasms
giving your gate
a ceremonial sway

A man and a woman
brought you here,
went back

A cross of ash
on a sexpot's
forehead

✡

No longer a lush but
those days remembered
as heaven on earth

No longer a thief but missing
such moments when
all seemed free

Manhattan no longer home
but every few blocks,
a liquor store

From his truck window
the one-legged gardener
pays back a loan

Left full at midnight
the wine glass a torch
in morning sun

Plates of steaks
at a pool party and
your father alive again

Soaked under a
gray sky the blossoms
seem more violet

Crestfallen and
weeping in
a field

☼

Nirvana exists
because few can bear
not to hear of it

Fire-breathing
skulls on the forearm of
a security guard

An end met amid
bare trees. Divine light
blurs the grotto

Come night,
all's quiet. Next
door, a cough

✧

The beauty of
the movie had you
wandering into sunlight in tears

When the couple
kissing on the grass
became shadows

Colors are
leaving the earth
Sun a final lick of fire

✡

God's thought in creating oceans:
that they should
taste of blood

✦

Sudden police boat cop flat on the deck
scanning under
the dock

Gleaming water
between the park and
the far dark

In dim light a police diver,
red wet suit, jumps
in and sinks

Medics, firemen,
rush to the far side of the pier
Fished-out body, alive

His belly rising
and falling, pale
and panting

Dogs, nannies, kids
at the rail, lining up and
looking down

A semidrowned man
drenched, eyes open
on a floating dock

Dropping, now, into
a deeper ocean,
the sky

Cops high-
fiving around
the gurney

Neck brace, mask, medic
kneeling, strapping
down his fidgets

A man, pulled up
breathless
from death,

eyes open,
wonderstruck
between sea and sky

CLOUDS OF THE REALM ABOVE

CLOUDS OF THE REALM ABOVE

Regardless, the earth
burns at the center
of the sun

A friend who died
is doing well at the tip of
Manhattan. He's opened a bar

Autumn advises:
Darken early. The leaves
urge: Oh, just go

Holes in the roof, drizzle
onto floorboards,
cold, unlit

A woman gently
washes ashes from
my eyelids

☼

Needing no elsewhere
yet needing not
to be here

Many who marveled
aloud at life, now silent,
in a dream

Or flail in a snowstorm, atop
a parking garage, locked
out of the car

The world of
quantifiable extension
is now just a casket showroom

At the medical tent
in a civic arena, it's getting
gladiatorial

Face purple,
undercoat of pink,
the drunk about to die

A shivering
pulls upward and away
into the blankets

Would you were the virgin
in robes of red, black, yellow,
and white, who says

"Lie down
in the dark amid
the crowd sprawled out

on the desanctified
cathedral floor. I will
let you discretely

stroke my long black
hair once the movie begins
on the screen behind the altar"

For a moment
the quiet goes calm
Early light feels pure

The base of the hill
all sunlight, the rise all
bands of shade

A once cogent
argument is now
pulled apart

☼

Debussy preferred
pleasure, did not like
pained states of being

He wanted chords to
meld and well and taper,
refraining from the

strife and crises of
the Austro-Hungarian
composers

He preferred the
immediacy of the
impermanent

☆

Thin orange horizon
Ecstasy turns to ocean
Dark pours in

A glow over the torn-up
driveway behind
the trees

Face showed no
upset but her throat
flushed red

A dancer held
to the earth
by black balloons

☼

I hand Hendrix
an amp wire, he, saying:
"We're all elsewhere"

As if on a subaquatic
volcano between two
continental plates

The rain stops
The glass of wine goes dry
I walk home on clear, wet streets

The air is pink
Ashes fill
every living lung

Love says: "Write as if
I'm here, but never
mention me"

☆

The painting feigns a fate
A flurry of triangles
ring a syllable

Walking a long while
in such cold who would not feel
dipped in flame?

Midmorning a metal roof
white in sunlight,
a snowfield

Having talked so
freely last night you
want your tongue cut out

A feeling, then, of
floating above or through
other people

Above or through
bent trees, broken stones,
stricken bodies, clouds

No rain fazes the
trotting dog, off-leash in
the amorous wet

✡

The meander
of a beggar down
an avenue of blossoms

One final time
the earth proves perfect
Soft, gray light

A Franciscan piety
not yet, it seems,
dead in you

A kiss so quick
no time to be
incredulous

☼

Tangled plasma
of the sun, driving
whales to suicide

✡

Once again, there, and
generous, the father
in a dream

Quiet, bright, cold,
glanced by light, rising
from dark, the island

While you're away
workmen install a glass
door in your house

An unknown
couple lets you hold,
for a moment, their newborn

Acknowledgments

An excerpt from "Infinite Criteria" appeared in *jubilat*.

About the Author

Joseph Donahue's most recent volumes of poetry are *Wind Maps I–VII* (Talisman 2018), and *The Disappearance of Fate*, (Spuyten Duyvil, 2019). He is the co-translator of *First Mountain*, by Zhang Er. With Edward Foster he edited *The World in Time and Space: Towards a History of Innovative American Poetry, 1970–2000* (Talisman, 2002). *Música Callada* and *Near Star*, two volumes in his ongoing poetic sequence, *Terra Lucida,* are forthcoming from Verge Books. Black Square Editions published *Red Flash on a Black Field* (2014).

Black Square Editions was started in 1999 with the intention of publishing translations of little-known books by well-known poets and fiction writers, as well as the work of emerging and established authors. After twenty-three years, we are still proceeding book by book.

Black Square Editions—a subsidiary of Off the Park Press, Inc., a tax-exempt (501c3) nonprofit organization—would like to thank the following for their support.

Tim Barry
Robert Bunker
Catherine Kehoe
Taylor Moore
Goldman Sachs
Pittsburgh Foundation Grant
Miles McEnery Gallery (New York, New York)
I.M. of Emily Mason & Wolf Kahn
Galerie Lelong & Co. (Paris, France)
Bernard Jacobson Gallery (London, England)
Saturnalia Books
& Anonymous Donors

Black Square Editions

Richard Anders *The Footprints of One Who Has Not Stepped Forth* (trans. Andrew Joron)

Andrea Applebee *Aletheia*

Eve Aschheim and Chris Daubert *Episodes with Wayne Thiebaud: Interviews*

Eve Aschheim *Eve Aschheim: Recent Work*

Anselm Berrigan *Pregrets*

Garrett Caples *The Garrett Caples Reader*

Marcel Cohen *Walls (Anamneses)* (trans. Brian Evenson and Joanna Howard)

Lynn Crawford *Fortification Resort*

Lynn Crawford *Simply Separate People, Two*

Thomas Devaney *You Are the Battery*

Ming Di (**Editor**) *New Poetry from China: 1917–2017* (trans. various)

Joseph Donahue *Red Flash on a Black Field*

Rachel Blau DuPlessis *Late Work*

Marcella Durand *To husband is to tender*

Rosalyn Drexler *To Smithereens*

Brian Evenson *Dark Property*

Serge Fauchereau *Complete Fiction* (trans. John Ashbery and Ron Padgett)

Jean Frémon *Painting* (trans. Brian Evenson)

Jean Frémon *The Paradoxes of Robert Ryman* (trans. Brian Evenson)

Ludwig Hohl *Ascent* (trans. Donna Stonecipher)

Isabelle Baladine Howald *phantomb* (trans. Eléna Rivera)

Philippe Jaccottet *Ponge, Pastures, Prairies* (trans. John Taylor)

Ann Jäderlund *Which once had been meadow* (trans. Johannes Göransson)

Franck André Jamme *Extracts from the Life of a Beetle* (trans. Michael Tweed)

Franck André Jamme *Another Silent Attack* (trans. Michael Tweed)

Franck André Jamme *The Recitation of Forgetting* (trans. John Ashbery)

Andrew Joron *Fathom*

Karl Larsson *FORM/FORCE* (trans. Jennifer Hayashida)

Hervé Le Tellier *Atlas Inutilis* (trans. Cole Swensen)

Eugene Lim *The Strangers*

Michael Leong *Cutting Time with a Knife*

Michael Leong *Words on Edge*

Gary Lutz *I Looked Alive*

Michèle Métail *Earth's Horizons: Panorama* (trans. Marcella Durand)

Michèle Métail *Identikits* (trans. Philip Terry)

Albert Mobilio *Me with Animal Towering*

Albert Mobilio *Touch Wood*

Albert Mobilio *Games & Stunts*

Albert Mobilio *Same Faces*

Pascalle Monnier *Bayart* (trans. Cole Swensen)

Christopher Nealon *The Joyous Age*

María Negroni *Berlin Interlude* (trans. Michelle Gil-Montero)

Doug Nufer *Never Again*

John Olson *Echo Regime*

John Olson *Free Stream Velocity*

Eva Kristina Olsson *The Angelgreen Sacrament* (trans. Johannes Göransson)

Juan Sánchez Peláez *Air on the Air: Selected Poems* (trans. Guillermo Parra)

Véronique Pittolo *Hero* (trans. Laura Mullen)

Pierre Reverdy *Prose Poems* (trans. Ron Padgett)

Pierre Reverdy *Haunted House* (trans. John Ashbery)

Pierre Reverdy *The Song of the Dead* (trans. Dan Bellm)

Pierre Reverdy *Georges Braque: A Methodical Adventure* (trans. Andrew Joron
   and Rose Vekony)

Valérie-Catherine Richez *THIS NOWHERE WHERE*

Barry Schwabsky *Book Left Open in the Rain*

Barry Schwabsky *Trembling Hand Equilibrium*

Barry Schwabsky *Heretics of Language*

Jeremy Sigler *Crackpot*

Jørn H. Sværen *Queen of England* (trans. Jørn H. Sværen)

Genya Turovskaya *The Breathing Body of This Thought*

Matvei Yankelevich *Some Worlds for Dr. Vogt*